Banjo Styles

by Larry Sandberg

©1978 Oak Publications

New York · London · Tokyo · Sydney · Cologne

Cover photos:
Tony Trischka by David Gahr
Art Rosenbaum by Margo Rosenbaum
Miles Krassen by Joe Holdner
Tim Jumper by Brian Misch

© Oak Publications, 1978
A Division of Embassy Music Corporation, New York
All Rights Reserved

International Standard Book Number: 0-8256-0225-4
Library of Congress Catalog Card Number: 77-95265

Distributed throughout the world by Music Sales Corporation:

33 West 60th Street, New York 10023

78 Newman Street, London W1

27 Clarendon Street, Artarmon, Sydney NSW

4-26-22 Jingumae, Shibuya-ku, Tokyo 150

Kölner Strasse 199, 5000 Cologne 90

Contents

Foreword

This book offers a sampling of the banjo player's delights found in the Oak/Acorn Publications collection of banjo books. It's a sort of smorgasbord: you can pick and choose your favorites, heaping your plate with appetizing goodies while you leave just a little room on the side for something new and strange-looking. And then, if you discover you like it, you can come back for seconds.

So here's hoping that this book will stimulate your appetite to search out new directions. It's arranged in an approximately progressive order of difficulty, so you can work your way through it or skip around as you find best. As for the lessons themselves, I'm proud to have had a hand in selecting them, and not too proud to say that I've learned a number of new things in the process.

A word about the authors whose selections are included here: Tim Jumper's approach is that of a conscientious teacher *par excellence*. Art Rosenbaum is a man who has engaged his entire personality in traditional music style. Tony Trischka is a true phenomenon, an avant-gardist in a traditional medium. Miles Krassen is a deep scholar of the music of the southern hill country, and of its English and Celtic antecedents. John Burke is a self-confessed "compulsive musician" who strives to keep old-time music alive and vital rather than imitatively stagnant. And Peter Wernick, a dedicated musician commited to social communication as well, possessess two important attributes of a bluegrass banjo player: he is both clever *and* funny. These are good men to learn from.

TUNINGS USED IN THIS BOOK

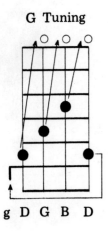

G Tuning

g D G B D

G Modal Tuning

g D G C D

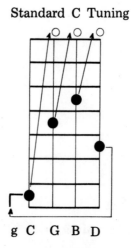

Standard C Tuning

g C G B D

Double C Tuning

g C G C D

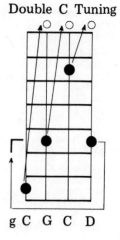

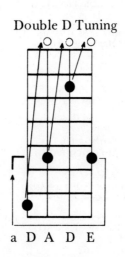

Open C Tuning

g C G C E

Double D Tuning

a D A D E

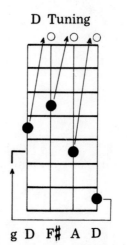

D Tuning

g D F♯ A D

(from *Melodic Banjo* by Tony Trischka)

You'll notice that some of the tablatures in this book have the fret numbers directly on the lines, while others use the spaces above the lines. Both systems are equally easy to follow. Additional symbols are:

I = index finger
M = middle finger
B = brush downwards (usually with middle finger)

R = roll downwards with 3rd, 2nd and 1st fingers
P = pull off
H = hammer on
S or SL = slide
PL = pluck string with a *left*-hand finger
CH or ↑ = "choke" or bend the string upwards in pitch
♩ , ♪ , or ⌐ = rest (play no note in that spot)

The music in this book will be written out in *tablature*. Tablature is a simple method of reading and writing music which applies specifically to the instrument for which it is written. You don't have to read music to understand it.

In our case, we'll be using a five line *staff*, with each line representing a string on the banjo:

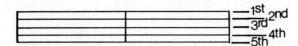

The vertical lines in the above example divide the staff into equal sections called measures. The length of the measure in a particular song is determined by the *time signature*. For instance, in bluegrass music—and in this book—most of the tunes are in 2/4 time. The 2 refers to the number of beats in each measure, and the 4 to the value of the beat. Thus in 2/4 time there are *two quarter* notes per measure.

This time signature can also be broken down to four eighth notes,

   or eight sixteenth notes:

In this book we'll generally be working with eight sixteenth notes per measure.

However, in tablature, numbers rather than notes are written on the lines of the staff to indicate what fret of which string is to be fingered by the left hand. For instance, to play the third fret of the second string you would find this notation:

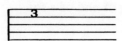

In the case of an open string, an "O" is used. An "X" on the middle line refers to a *rest* (or space where no note is played) equal in value to the other notes in the measure.

Underneath each number is an indication as to how the right hand will pick that note:

      T = thumb
      1 = index finger
      2 = middle finger

Here's an example:

T 1 2 T 2 1 T 2

repeat sign

The signs

 and

mean that you should repeat the section enclosed by them. In most cases in this book, you'll be repeating entire verses or choruses. If there is no

before the final

you should go back to the beginning of the section. When the section to be repeated has two separate endings, it is indicated like this:

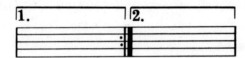

This means that you should play through the entire section once, using the first ending; then go back to the beginning and play it through again, this time skipping the first ending and playing the second one.

triplets

A triplet is a group of three notes which is performed in the same length of time as two. You can use it most effectively to give a little extra push to the beginning or end of a song. Here's how a triplet looks in tablature:

T 1 2

Mountain and Old-Time Style and Technique

FRAILING
(from *How to Play Banjo* by Tim Jumper)
No one seems to know where the strange word "frailing" comes from, but everyone recognizes its sound in the bouncy beat of mountain banjo music. Here's an exposition of the basic rhythmic gesture, followed by its application in "Buffalo Gals" and "Waterbound." Tune to G tuning (gDGBD).

The Frailing Stroke

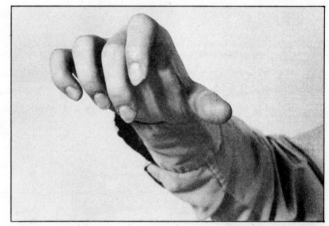

Hold your hand in a claw-like position over the strings with your middle finger extended a little beyond the others.

Pick the first string with the back of the middle fingernail using a motion from the wrist and forearm as if you were rapping on a table. The hand moves *down*—toward the floor—and *in*—toward the banjo head. Don't flick the middle finger out. Maintain the claw position and on the follow-through let the middle fingernail actually hit the banjo head after sounding the first string.

Having picked the first string, your hand should seem to bounce off the banjo head to be in position for the strum. The basic frailing rhythm is exactly the same as that of up-picking.

Play this over and over until you get a good clear sound with an even steady beat.

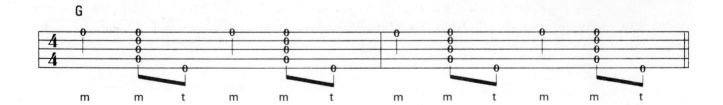

Hint—Let your middle fingernail grow out a little beyond the fleshy tip of your finger. This will make it easier to sound the melody note cleanly and crisply. If you can't keep a longer nail on the middle finger, a light guage metal fingerpick can be used. It's not as good as a natural nail but it will serve the purpose.

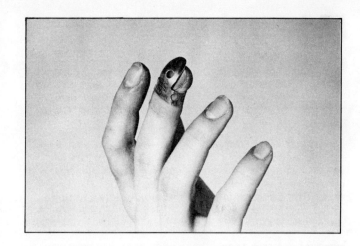

Buffalo Gals

Buf - fa - lo ___ gals won't you come out ___ to-night Won't you come out tonight Won't you come out ___ to-night ___

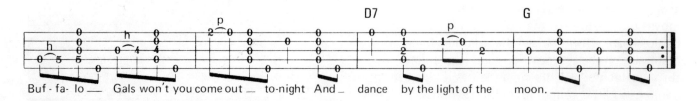

Buf - fa - lo ___ Gals won't you come out ___ to-night And ___ dance by the light of the moon. ___

Waterbound

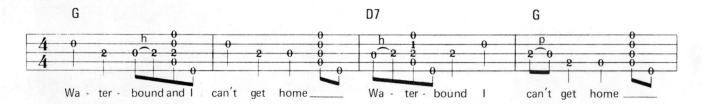

Wa - ter - bound and I can't get home ___ Wa - ter - bound I can't get home ___

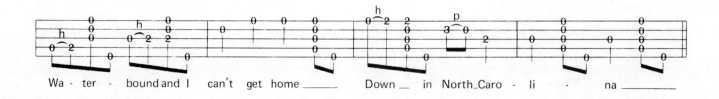

Wa - ter - bound and I can't get home ___ Down ___ in North Caro - li - na

MORE DOWN-PICKING
(from *Old-Time Mountain Banjo* by Art Rosenbaum)
The basic frailing stroke can be varied to produce an amazing number of different sounds, rhythms, and textures.
Art Rosenbaum offers "Black-Eyed Suzie" to demon-
strate some of these possibilities. Tune to double C tuning (gCGCD).

CLAWHAMMER, DROP THUMB, FRAILING

There is a great family of down-picking styles in the South known variously as knocking, knock-
down, drop-thumb, beating, rapping, clawhammer, flyin' hand, framming, or frailing. These are
local names and do not necessarily refer to stylistic differences, although these differences exist
a-plenty. The same basic approach to sounding a banjo--striking downward--can from player to
player and from region to region produce a wide range of sounds. It can give a song a simple
rippling accompaniment or an intricate one, weaving complex figures among or between phrases
sung by the voice; it can create driving mountain dance music either alone or with the fiddle
and other instruments. It can be highly percussive in character, although in certain areas talent-
ed musicians have created styles in which the banjo rivals the fiddle in ability to carry a melodic
line.

I'll assume that you have acquired the rudiments of down-picking in the first chapter of this
book or elsewhere. In either case glance back over that section before you proceed, because
the hints I have given on hand position and attack will make the material in the present chapter much easier to learn. That material is simply an exploration of some of the different sounds
made possibly by down-picking with some examples pointing up regional differences or illustrating the styles of some of the old-time pickers whose music has become known through recordings.

RHYTHM DROP-THUMB

Once your right hand can effortlessly knock out a clean down-picking rhythm and incorporate
hammers, pulls, and slides into the pattern to carry a melody, you can add the next ingredient,
the *drop-thumb*, which is the equivalent of *double thumbing* in the up-picking style. Do you
recall how the thumb followed *every* strong beat in the first stage of *Hook and Line*? In that
example the thumb stayed on the 5th string. Then we eliminated it after the first beat to make
this basic pattern:

But the thumb trails along with the hand as it comes down, so it
can just as easily do this again:

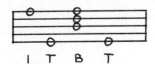

I T B T

Or, instead of hitting the 5th string on the first off-beat, it can drop down to the 2nd string:

I T I T

The brush is eliminated in favor of another index note on the 1st string, but this should present no problem.

Just remember that the thumb drops to rest on the second string *at the same instant* that the first note is sounded, not even a split second after. Then the thumb flexes and sounds the 2nd string as the hand bounces up into position to descend again. Then the hand comes down, the index striking the 1st string as the thumb comes to rest on the 5th string. Finally the 5th string is sounded. Once you have mastered this simple sequence you will be able to vary the order of the strings in ways which will be explained later. But first, try a tune in the old-time breakdown or square dance style that uses a lot of this rhythm drop-thumb. That is, the thumb alternates between the 5th and the second string for rhythmic purposes as the index lead carries the melody.

Stephan Wade

BLACK-EYED SUSIE

PART I

Susie, keep them hoe-cakes a-bakin', sold my fiddle to buy some bacon.
Ducks in the mill-pond, geese in the clover, tell them pretty girls I'm comin' over!

PART II

Hey pretty little black-eyed Susie, hey pretty little black-eyed Susie (2)

All I want in this creation,
Pretty little wife and a big plantation.

PART II:

Hey, pretty little black-eyed Susie, (2x)
Hey, pretty little black-eyed Susie, hey!

All I need to make me happy,
Two little boys to call me Pappy—
One named Sop; one named Davy;
One loves meat and the other loves gravy.

Susie and the boys went huckleberry pickin',
The boys got drunk and Susie got a lickin'.

This is not the most intricate or subtle sort of banjo piece but it has a good solid rhythm and could be continued for a half an hour or so while the dancers go through the figures of a running set. It follows, incidentally, the two-part form of most British and American fiddle tunes.

I have heard some old timers play who didn't consider it wrong to hit more than one string on the main accents, creating this kind of full sound:

CLAWHAMMER

(from *How to Play Banjo* by Tim Jumper)
Clawhammer style, as the old-timers call it, substitutes a single note for the brush in frailing. It's a pretty fair trade-off: you lose some bounce and gain some grace; you lose some harmony and gain more melodic shape. The style works beautifully in the two fiddle tunes that Jumper has selected, "June Apple" and "Sandy River Belle." Tune to G tuning (gDGBD).

A more refined type of frailing is known variously as *drop-thumb frailing, melodic frailing, strumless frailing,* or simply, *clawhammer.* The differences between frailing and clawhammer are subtle but unmistakeable once your ear is attuned to them. In frailing the melody generally alternates with chords, i.e. strums, whereas in clawhammer the emphasis is on linear melody with few chord-strums. The following examples point out the main differences between the two styles.

In clawhammer fewer strums are used.

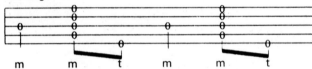

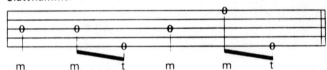

Clawhammer uses more varieties of drop-thumbing.

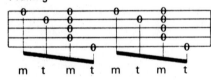

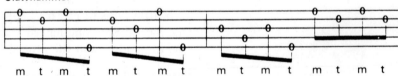

Clawhammer frequently uses drop-thumbing instead of pulling-off.

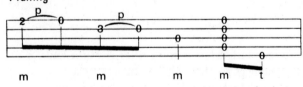

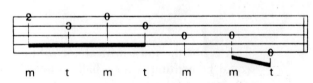

In clawhammer the fifth string is often used as a melody note. Notice also that it is a quarter note.

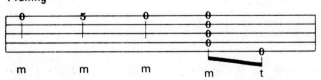

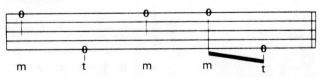

June Apple

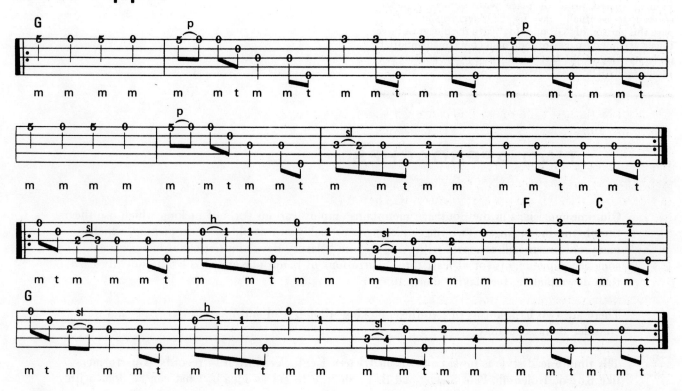

Sandy River Belle

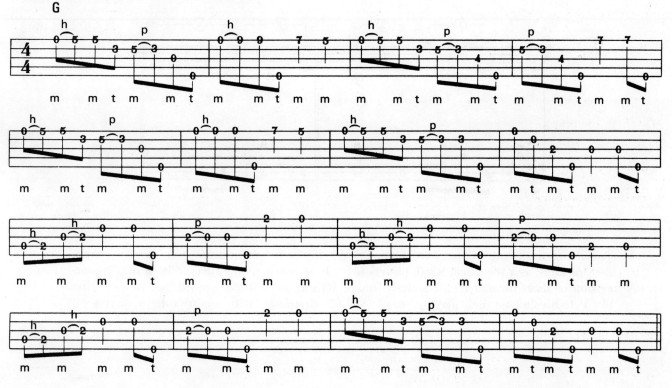

TWO-FINGER PICKING
(from *Old-Time Mountain Banjo* by Art Rosenbaum)
Frailing shared pride of place with numerous picking styles that eventually gave us the bluegrass sound. Compare this verison of "Ground Hog" with the bluegrass three-finger version on page 46, and you'll come to an important understanding of the history of banjo picking. Tune to G tuning (gDGBD).

TWO APPROACHES

Old-time musicians in the Southern mountains employ various sorts of picking which use the thumb and index finger. Two-finger picking is probably not as old as down-picking, which many old-timers still associate with Ante Bellum "slavery days" music; but it has provided song accompaniments for at least three generations of banjo players (it is less frequently used than down-picking for playing dance tunes.)

There are two basic forms of two-finger picking—thumb lead and index finger lead—and we'll consider them separately.

The thumb lead style is most common in Eastern Kentucky. Listen to records of performers like Roscoe Holcomb, Pete Steele, and B. F. Shelton to get an idea of what can be done with it.

Here are the basic mechanics: the right hand is held in place with the three fingers not used braced on the head while the thumb alternates between a lead on the inside strings and the fifth string and the index carries on a drone on the first string sounded on the off-beats. Try these patterns:

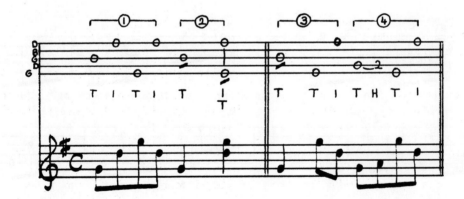

This is practically all you need to know. Try playing each half measure over and over—then each measure as a sequence. Some players use 1 as the basis for their style—a rippling succession of short notes with the melody finding its way in on the thumbed lead notes. Others like Pete Steele base their playing on 1 and 2 combined, with a more intense driving effect resulting from the syncopation of the final pinch of the outside strings. Pattern 3 provides a ♩♫ BUMP-ditty rhythm, and 4 adds the fluidity of a hammer or a pull to a style based on any of the other patterns or to any combination. Here is how a simple tune might sound in a two-finger style:

GROUND HOG

Whet up your ax and whistle up your dog, (2)
We're off to the woods to ketch a ground hog,
  Ground hog!

Old Joe Digger, Sam and Dave, (2)
Went a-hog huntin' hard as they could stave,
  Ground hog!

Down the holler and up the side, (2)
Y' get ten cents for the ground hog hide,
  Ground hog!

Up run Sam with a forked pole, (2)
To twist that ground hog out-a his hole,
  Ground hog!

Sam held the gun and Dave pulled the trigger, (2)
But the one killed the hog was old Joe Digger,
  Ground hog!

Up come Suzie with a snigger and a grin, (2)
Ground hog grease all over her chin,
  Ground hog!

Old Aunt Sally was the mother of 'em all, (2)
Fed 'em on ground hog before they could crawl,
  Ground hog!

The vocal melody here pretty much follows the thumb notes on the inside strings. If you are familiar with this tune try varying the style, favoring one or another pattern, adding hammers or pulls—just be careful to preserve the melody (or a variant that you may know) and the metric structure.

Bluegrass Style and Technique

ROLLS
(from *How to Play Banjo* by Tim Jumper)
The most readily identifiable sound in bluegrass music is the banjo sound named Scruggs-picking after its best-known and greatest exponent. Earl Scruggs' style is based on a series of thumb, middle- and index-finger gestures called **rolls**. Here Tim Jumper shows how they combine to produce music in "Worried Man Blues" and "Will the Circle Be Unbroken." Tune to G Tuning (gDGBD).

Concentrate on maintaining the correct right hand position while you try this exercise a few times.

Are you getting a clear sound from each string? All the notes are eighth notes and, when correctly played, produce an even-sounding *roll,* or flow of notes which is the essence of the bluegrass sound.

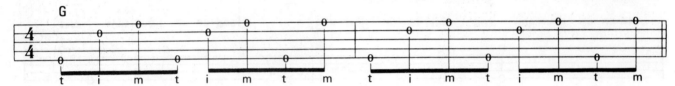

Rolls

A roll is a series of notes picked by the right hand fingers in a recognizable pattern. Mastery of the basic rolls is the foundation of bluegrass banjo playing. The one you just played is called a *foward roll.* Here are two others, called *reverse rolls.*

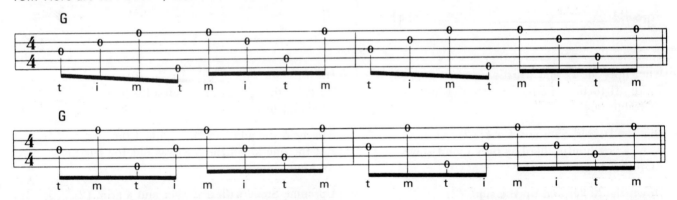

Notice how these same two rolls can be used to pick a different combination of strings.

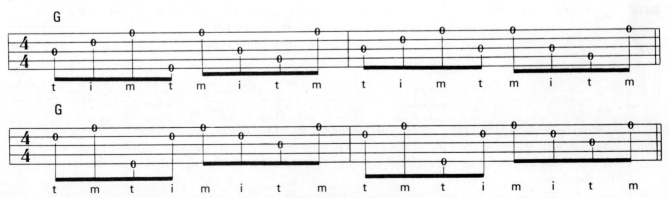

16

Try playing these rolls with the C and D7 chords. Aim for a clear, flowing sound. Don't worry about speed right now. Concentrate on accuracy and keeping the beat. Speed will come naturally with practice.

Hint—When playing, don't let your thumb drift back toward your palm and fingers. Maintain the correct right hand position. It will aid your progress.

A Bluegrass Solo

Here is a tune in the bluegrass style using the rolls you have learned. Most of the melody notes in a bluegrass solo are picked by the thumb, so stress the thumb notes, except for those on the fifth string.

Earl Scruggs

Worried Man Blues

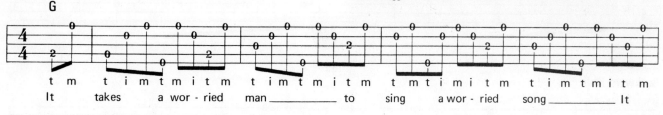

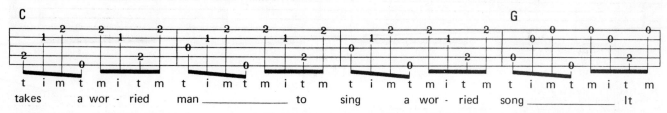

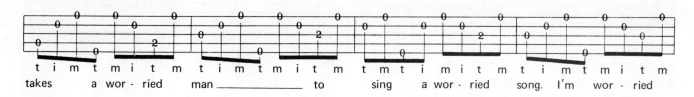

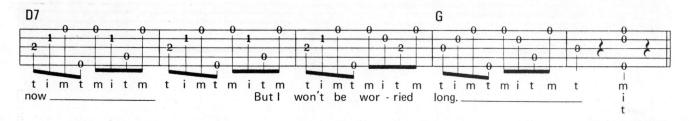

More Rolls

Here are some other common rolls. Try them with C and D7 as well as G, and don't be afraid to experiment with various string combinations.

Forward Roll

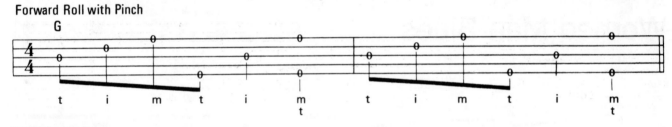

Forward Roll

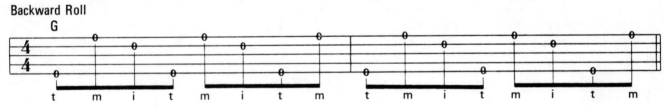

Forward Roll with Pinch

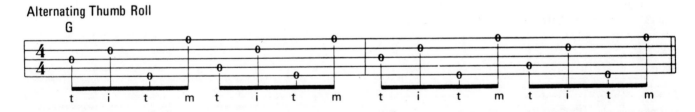

Backward Roll

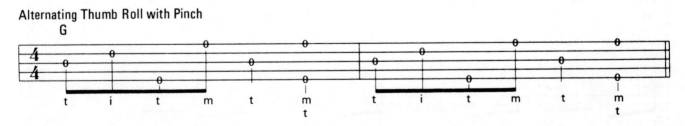

Alternating Thumb Roll

Alternating Thumb Roll with Pinch

18

Will The Circle Be Unbroken

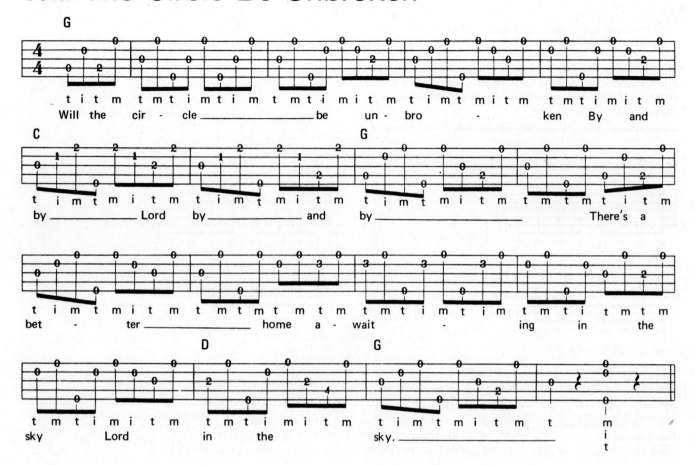

UNORTHODOX ROLLS
(from *Bluegrass Banjo* by Peter Wernick)
What Wernick has in mind is your conversion from a basically adequate Scruggs-style player to an interesting one, for as you increase your repertory of rolls you can put melody notes in a greater variety of places. With "In My Mind to Ramble" and "Old Joe Clark" you can learn to control phrasing and transcend limitations in technique. Tune to G tuning (gDGBD).

Here are four rolls that start with the middle finger:

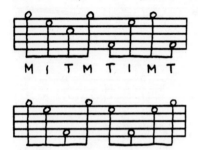

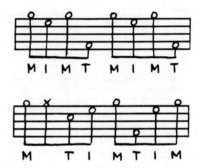

There is no need to memorize these rolls, but it would be a good exercise to go through each one until you can play it comfortably. If your hand has difficulty getting accustomed to starting a roll with the middle finger, that's all the more reason to practice them. Your right hand should eventually learn to be comfortable with *any* sequence. If you can loosen up your right hand so that it can pick up and adapt to a pattern quickly, many new possibilities are opened to you. To see what I mean, play each of the four rolls I have just given you on a simple D7 chord. Each one has a markedly different sound, and it all happens using just one simple left hand formation. Imagine what can happen when you apply a wide variety of right hand patterns to a wide variety of left hand ideas! Endless possibilities. Another thought which may inspire you to work on loosening up your right hand: Melodic style banjo ("chromatic", "Keith style") requires the right hand to be able to play any sequence of strings rapidly and flawlessly.

Here are two more rolls to practice. They both start with the index finger *followed by the thumb* (not beginning with the thumb, as you have been doing so far).

Next, three licks using a new right hand variation: the middle finger hitting the second string. These licks all sound particularly good if the right hand is far enough from the bridge to create a mellow tone, enabling the notes to blend together nicely.

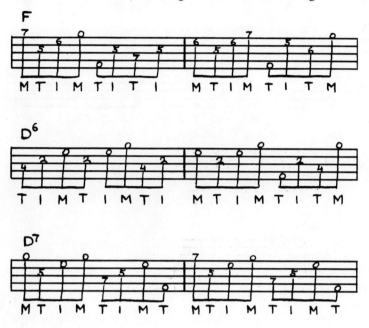

Now here are two arrangements which use some of the right hand ideas you haven't encountered in any of the arrangements I've given to you so far.

In My Mind to Ramble

Peter Wernick
As played by Bill Runkle on Del McCoury's *High On a Mountain* album on Rounder.
© Copyright 1974 by Peter Wernick.
All Rights Reserved. Used by Permission.

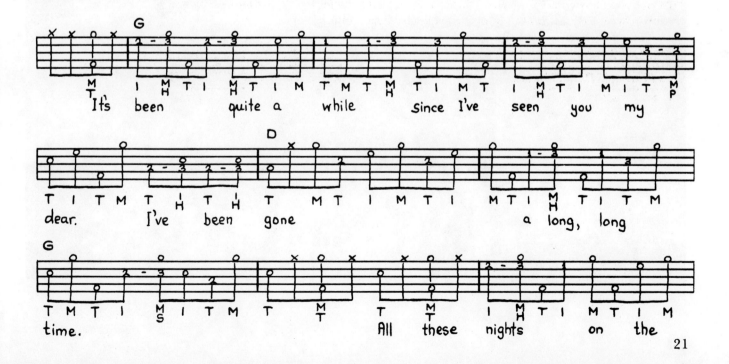

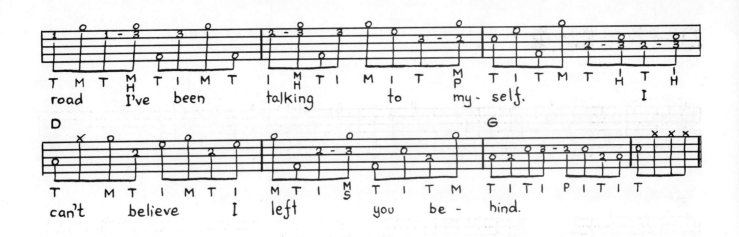

road I've been   talking   to   my- self.   I

can't believe I   left   you be - hind.

Flatt and Scruggs and the Foggy Mt. Boys

22

Old Joe Clark

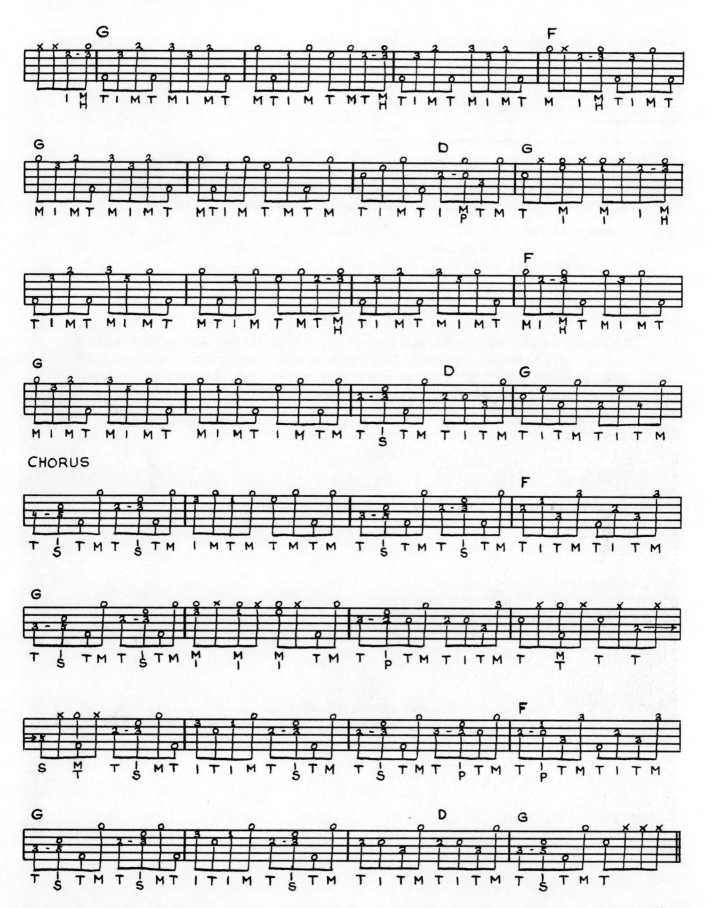

THE MELODIC STYLE

(from *Melodic Banjo* by Tony Trischka)

The melodic style is the most exciting new development in banjo playing since Earl Scruggs made his initial impact more than three decades ago. It's somewhat analogous to clawhammer style in that it modifies an existing traditional technique in order to express melodies more efficiently. In this case, the style modifies the basic rolls of Scruggs-picking in an even more extreme fashion, at the same time calling on a more complex left-hand technique, in order to achieve melodic results in a brilliant picking style. Tune to G tuning (gDGBD).

The key to the melodic style is the idea that you *never* pick the same string twice in a row. By alternating strings, many of them open, you can get a smooth, rolling sound.

Instead of playing, you can play:

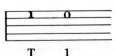 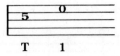

To expand on this idea, here are two versions of a G scale, the first done in the Reno style and the second, melodically. Notice that the Reno style only uses the thumb and index finger of the right hand, while the melodic style uses the thumb, index and middle fingers. This allows for greater versatility and speed in playing.

Reno style:

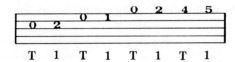

Melodic style:

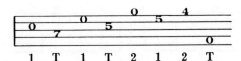

You'll find that when you fret a string in the melodic style, it's often higher in pitch than the next higher open string. For instance, the third string - fifth fret produces a higher note than the open second string. This phenomenon may be hard to get used to at first, but after a little bit of practice, it'll get much easier.

We've now compared the melodic approach to Reno picking, but how does it differ from Scruggs style? In the melodic style, most of the notes played are melody notes. Scruggs style, on the other hand, has its basis in chords, so it can only approximate the melody. This is especially true in the case of fiddle tunes. Listen to Scruggs' playing on "Sally Goodin" from *Foggy Mountain Banjo* (CS - 8364), and compare it to the version included on the record in this book. Scruggs only plays every third or fourth melody note, while the notes he puts in-between serve as embellishment. In the melodic version, all the melody notes are included and given equal clarity and importance.

Also, in Scruggs style the right hand usually emphasizes only the melody notes, while it skims over the others in a sort of chordal wash. In the melodic approach, where all the notes are part of the melody, the accents fall in a variety of places, depending on the mood of the musician and the nature of the tune. This all has to do with *dynamics*, or the stressing of one note or passage over another, in order to make the music more expressive.

One other difference between the two styles has to do with the role of the fifth string. Scruggs uses it mostly as a drone and rarely frets it except to add color to backup chords. In the melodic style, the fifth string is often fretted and becomes important as an equal carrier of the melody. Here's an example:

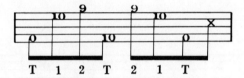

Before we get into heavy playing in the chapters ahead, I'd like to discuss one more thing with you—rhythm. Melodic playing involves a set of right hand rolls that aren't always found in Scruggs style, and until you get used to them your time may be a little shaky. For this reason I suggest that you work with a metronome. This will involve a certain amount of patience and discipline on your part; but if you can play along slowly with the metronome as you're learning new licks or songs and gradually work up to faster tempos, you'll find an amazing improvement in your rhythm. Remember, a steady rhythm is one of the most important elements you can have in your playing.

Now that you've gone through a few scales you can put them to practical use. Here's how Bill applied them to his music: "The first use I made of this technique to play licks like this was:

and

Both of these runs fit nicely into this melodic version of "Cripple Creek":

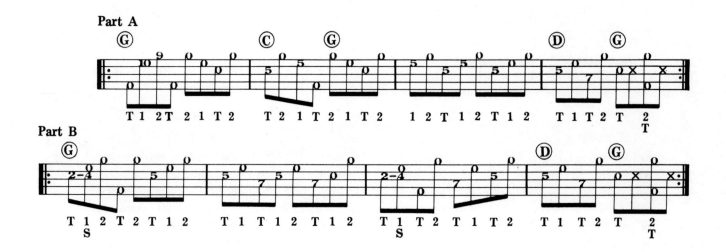

THREE-QUARTER TIME

(from *Bluegrass Banjo* by Peter Wernick)
A good country waltz like "All the Good Times" is always
fun to play and sing, but too many banjo players miss out
on the good times because they've neglected to learn to
adapt the bluegrass roll to a three-beat feeling. Here's how.
Tune to G tuning (gDGBD).

A small percentage of bluegrass songs are in 3/4 time. Rarely is 3/4 time used in anything but
slow songs, and since banjo is infrequently used for lead on slow songs you will hardly ever
have to do a lead in 3/4. But of course you should be prepared for whatever comes along, and
playing backup and occasionally lead in 3/4 time will come along.

The phrase 3/4 time means the rhythm goes "boom-chick-chick, boom-chick-chick". Fast
bluegrass is in 2/4 time ("boom-chick, boom-chick") and most slow bluegrass is in 4/4 time
("boom-chick-chick-chick, boom-chick-chick-chick"). Sometimes 3/4 time is called waltz
rhythm – waltzes are always played in that time because the dance involves one big step
and two smaller ones.

Backup for a slow song in 3/4 means following along with the "boom-chick-chick", especially the "boom" which you'll usually find yourself playing with the thumb. As with slow
songs in 4/4 time, you don't play rolls, just go at it in an open-ended way with the aim of
doing what you can to contribute to a good overall band sound.

Here is the basic right hand pattern for 3/4 time:

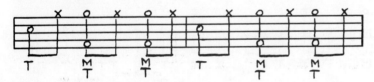

Or to fill up more spaces, any of these three patterns:

  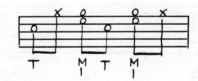

The main thing to keep in mind is that you now have six spaces, not eight, to fill up a measure. If you play along with records in 3/4 time, you'll probably fall into simple ideas after
a while. Some examples of well-known songs in 3/4 are *Tennessee Waltz, Shenendoah Waltz*
(or any other waltz), *All the Good Times Are Past and Gone, White Dove, Ocean of Dia-
monds, That Was Before I Met You,* and the first half of *Blue Moon of Kentucky* (which
then speeds up into a brisk 2/4).

Every now and then a song in 3/4 is fast enough to make it worthwhile for the banjo to play
rolls. Playing rolls in 3/4 is weird at first because the rolls have to be six notes long and not
eight. Here are some sample six-note rolls:

 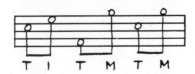

 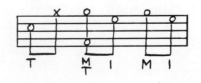

The most popular 3/4 song suited to playing rolls is *All the Good Times Are Past and Gone* which is not only a standard, but one in which the banjo is often given a chance to play lead. Here is an arrangement of this song:

All the Good Times Are Past and Gone

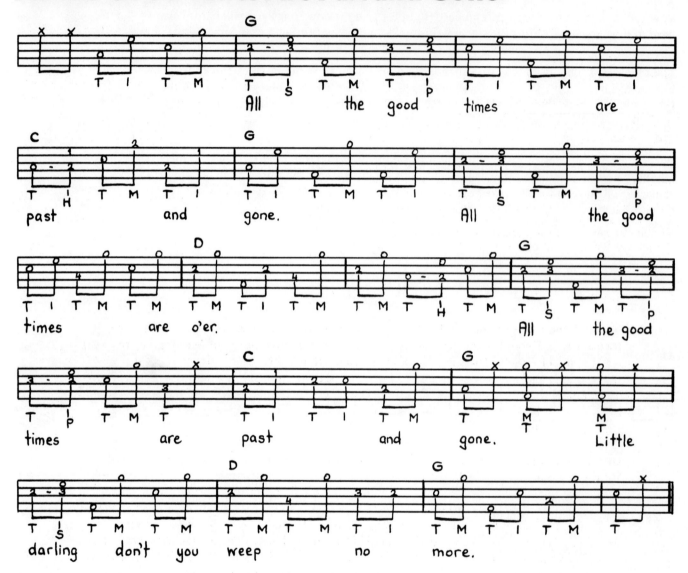

The Soul of Old-Time and Mountain Music

VARIATION AND IMPROVISATION

(from *Old-Time Mountain Banjo* by Art Rosenbaum)

Do you know the story of the grizzled veteran who told the technical whiz kid, "You've got plenty of hot licks but no character in your style, and I bet your own mother couldn't recognize you on the radio." The style of a true master is as personal and unique (and as recognizable) as his voice. It comes as the result of many choices and decisions, some conscious and some not.

The treatment and phrasing of melody is one of the most important characteristics of a personal style. (The others are touch and tone.) Rosenbaum's treatment of "Old Ruben" is an especially valuable illustration of his sound advice on variation. By combining various sources into a set of variations he teaches you to put things together in new ways. This is what you must be doing, constantly and throughout your musical life, whenever you hear a new tune or a new version of an old tune. In this way, by feeling out what to accept and what to reject, you can incorporate elements of newness and self-expression within the acceptable limits of traditional style. Tune to D tuning (f♯ DF♯ AD).

Many of the tunes in this book are as close to note for note transcriptions of actual performances as I could make. The student should have no qualms about learning by following a good model closely; traditional musicians, too, often try to "get it down just like" an admired player picks a particular tune. This is not slavish imitation for its own sake but rather a passionate desire to get at the very sinews of the style, based on the realization that the impact of traditional music depends on detail and an evocative context, i.e. a particularly moving performance.

Of course the student is aware of the fact that folk musicians, like Rufus Crisp or Paul Joines or Buell Kazee or Clarence Ashley or Samantha Bumgarner, have or had a personal expressive quality or sound based on technical factors like certain preferred tunings, licks, figures, general touch and attack, choice of repertoire, and on each individual personality; the student is naturally desirous of making his own statement with the music rather than crawling into someone else's artistic skin. This is fine as long as one appreciates the fact that folk styles tend to be conservative and one doesn't have to move the earth in order to express oneself *within* a tradition. A little personal innovation goes a long way in this music and one needn't go overboard in the direction of technical virtuosity, self-consciously weird harmonic effects, or jazz-inspired no-holds-barred" improvisations on the theme" to add something of oneself to traditional banjo playing.

But what role do variation and improvisation play in mountain banjo music and how is the student to put them to use? It is important to understand that the first banjo player to try his hand at *The Soldier's Joy* had the fiddle tune in his head and improvised his way through the melody and rhythm by experimentation with the various techniques at his command. And at each succeeding go-round this man and his musical heirs varied the treatment to suit themselves and their listeners, preserving what they found satisfying. A similar process was followed for setting the old unaccompanied ballads to banjo. A lot of listening will give you a sense of how much variation goes on during a given performance and a sense of what kind of variation fits with the style. Of course some players do quite a lot, while others are content to play the tune pretty similarly each time.

To give you an idea of what can be done with a simple tune try these variations on *Old Ruben*. It is a *potpourri* taken from the playing of Wade Ward, Riley Shelton, Cass Moore, Pete Steele, and Vester Jones and has much more than any one player would put into a performance—but it is all good banjo stuff.

OLD RUBEN

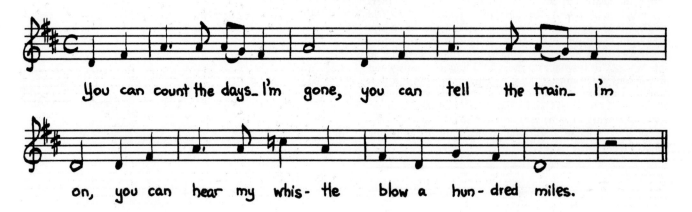

You can count the days I'm gone, you can tell the train I'm on, you can hear my whis-tle blow a hun-dred miles.

Down in seaport city, was a sportin' little town,
The dudes all a-standin' around.
Well, the chief of police and the captain too,
Drove them dudes right out of town.

Old Ruben, oh, Ru–, Ruben, oh, Ru–,
Well, it's Ruben, where you been so long?

Been to the east, been to the west,
Goin' where those chilly winds don't blow.

If the train runs me right, be home tomorrow night,
I'm five hundred miles from my home.

A rudimentary banjo melody could be played in the D tuning without the use of the left hand, illustrating the principle that tunings often include many of the melody notes of a given piece (granted this is stretching things a bit).

31

SOURWOOD MOUNTAIN AND JOHN HENRY
(from *John Burke's Book of Old-Time Fiddle Tunes for Banjo*)
Wade Ward was one of our finest banjo players, and a fiddler to boot. Burke's comments on simplicity in Ward's playing should never be forgotten. The awesome strength of a player like Ward comes not from technical display but from a sense of *rightness* that permeates every sound, every move, every decision. "John Henry" comes from Tom Paley, a former New Lost City Rambler whose sense of traditional rightness is exemplary among urban players.
For "Sourwood Mountain" tune to G tuning (gDGBD).
For "John Henry" tune to open C tuning (gCGCE).

Sourwood Mountain

G D G B D

from WADE WARD

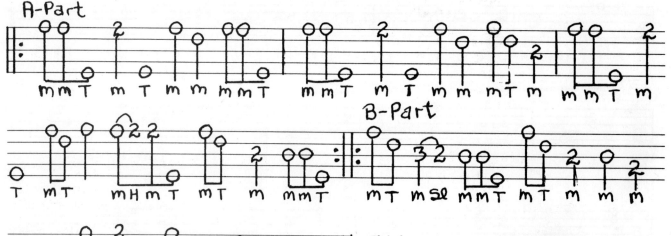

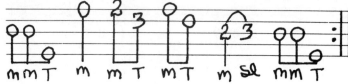

Chickens grow on Sourwood Mountain,
Hey, ho, hum diddle aye day,
So many pretty girls I can't count them,
Hey, ho, diddle aye day.

Reference:
Folkways: Roscoe Holcomb & Wade Ward
FA 2363
Traditional Music: Grayson &
Carroll Counties. FS3811A

This tune is most often done with the fiddle and banjo together - a good combination. It is written here as played by Wade Ward and you can see that it keeps the melody very simple. You need good, clean slides and precise one-note-at-a-time picking.

There is no need to obscure a pretty melody with fancy picking. A good tune rendered simply is always preferable to a conglomeration of intricate, hastily performed effects. A good musician always tries to give a sense of the tune's beauty rather than leave them gasping.

John Henry

G C G C E

from TOM PALEY

A-Part

Reference:
Elektra Records: Folk Banjo Styles
ELK217

The section marked "R" should be replaced with "S" the last time you play the piece through. I always considered Tom to be one of two or three best banjo players from the city. His setting of this well-known piece is one of his best.

Winnie Winston did a recording of it for Elektra Records on The Old Time Banjo Project in which he played an F chord in the section I have marked "N" by barring at the fifth fret.

ANGELINE AND SALLY ANN
(from *Clawhammer Banjo* by Miles Krassen)
Two popular fiddle tunes in double D tuning (aDADE). This is the way the old-timers tuned their banjos in order to play along with a fiddler without having to use a capo (capos were scarce in the mountains). City folks often find it easier to tune to double C tuning (gCGCD) and capo to the second fret. You can read the tablature either way without making any changes.

Angeline

Frank George plays *Angeline* on his Kanawha record with Pat Dunford on the banjo. This record is probably responsible for the tune's current popularity as it is now being played everywhere between New England and California. Uncle Eck Dunford recorded a version with words as Angeline the Baker. See *Appalachian Fiddle* for a fiddle version.

Sally Ann

A tune by the same name with a similar melody exists which is played in the key of A. But around Galax, I have always heard *Sally Ann* played in D. Fred Price fiddled a version with Clarence Ashley for Folkways. Sidna and Fulton Myers of Virginia have also recorded an old-time version. The best rendition I ever heard was by Wade Ward with Charlie Higgins fiddling.

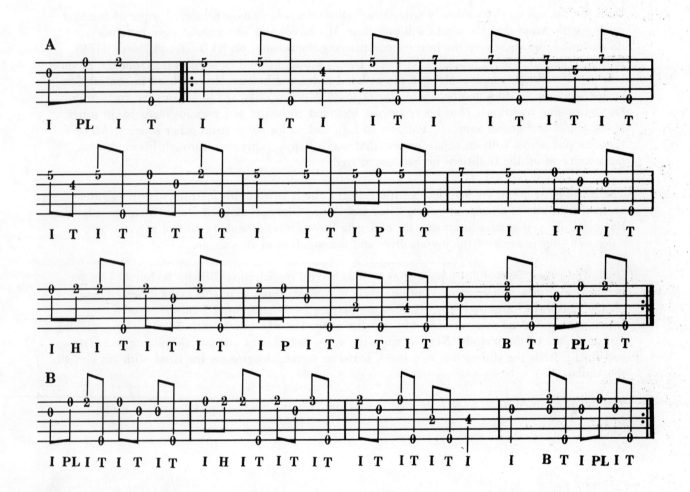

UNCLE DAVE MACON

(from *Old-Time Mountain Banjo* by Art Rosenbaum)
Uncle Dave, who died in 1955, was a legend of the early days of the Grand Old Opry broadcasts from Nashville. "Way Down the Old Plank Road" takes you through a whole gamut of banjo styles that typifies Uncle Dave's exuberant versatility. Tune to open C tuning (gCGCE).

Dave Macon was an extraordinary entertainer whose recordings have preserved some of the best singing with banjo that the world will ever hear. His career and background have been ably documented elsewhere (see the notes accompanying the reissues on RFB 51 and Decca 4760). It should be noted here, though, that Uncle Dave's music differed in some ways from the mountain banjo tradition which evolved in the isolated coves and hollers. He was born in central Tennessee, grew up in show business, and was exposed from an early age to various Negro instrumental and singing traditions. Thus his repertoire included authentic and pseudo-Negro banjo songs, blues, comic and gospel songs, in addition to folk and parlor songs from other sources. All of these he put across with an expansiveness that was a happy expression through his exuberant personality of all the traditions he had assimilated.

The learning banjo picker may feel a little reticent about twirling his instrument through the air in the middle of a song, or yelling "Hot Dog!" or "Glory, Hallelujah Damn!" during a break. But certainly you should listen to a lot of Uncle Dave's records and try to feel in your own voice and fingers some of the joyous drive and syncopation of this music.

Uncle Dave used frailing down-picking as well as several unorthodox 3-finger techniques on the banjo. Sometimes he used more than one style in a single song, as in *Old Plank Road,* reissued on the Folkways Anthology Vol. III. First he plays a freely-structured 3-finger introduction which anticipates the main melodic ideas of the song. Then he breaks into down-picking, playing the verse part of the melody. Next he sings the verse and chorus, alternately picking and frailing, and finally frails the chorus line as a break between verses, clogging on the floor with his feet all the while.

The banjo is tuned in an open C tuning. (From the 2C tuning, raise the 1st string a whole tone, to E.)

WAY DOWN THE OLD PLANK ROAD

Notice the figure in the 14th measure of the introduction where four picked notes are clustered into the space of one beat. This is the 3-finger counterpart of the roll in downpicking.

VOCAL LINE (BANJO AD LIB.)

1. Rath-er be in Rich-mond 'midst all the hail and rain, than for to be in Geor- gia boys wear- in' that ball_ and chain! Won't_ get drunk no more! Won't get drunk no more! Won't get drunk no more, way down on Plank Road.

CHORUS:

Right into break

I went down to Mobile for to get on the gravel train,
Very next thing they heard of me had on the ball
and chain!

Joanie, oh, dear Joanie, what makes you treat me so?
Caused me to wear the ball and chain now my
ankle's sore!

Knoxville is a pretty burg, Memphis is a beauty;
'F you want to see those pretty girls, hop to
Chattanoogie!

I'm gwine build me a scaffold upon the mountain
high,
As I can see the Laura girl as she goes ridin' by.

My wife died Friday night, Saturday she was buried;
Sunday was my courting day, Monday I got married.

Eighteen pounds of meat a week, whiskey here to
sell.
How can a young man stay at home, pretty girls look
so well!

BREAK (Down picking)

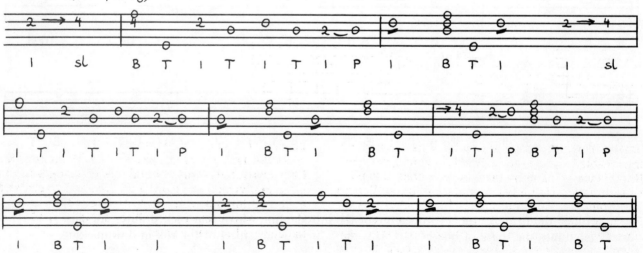

CHARLIE POOLE

(from *Banjo Songbook* by Tony Trischka)

Poole (like Snuffy Jenkins, p. 41) was a key figure in the transition from old-time to bluegrass style. A ruinous lifestyle undid his early rise to stardom, but he left a legacy of fine solos on traditional tunes like "Flop Eared Mule," as well as many original comic songs that are still sung today. Tune to G tuning (gDGBD).

Charlie Poole is probably the most well-known of all the old-time three-finger players. His style, like that of Frank Jenkins, is especially noteworthy because it bridged the gaps between classic, old time, and bluegrass banjo.

Charlie was born on March 22, 1892 in Spray, North Carolina, and grew up in impoverished circumstances. In fact, when his father decided to move from one part of the country to another, a wagon was used instead of a truck to carry the family belongings. At age ten, Charlie set out on his own to learn the banjo. He didn't have the benefit of records to listen to because in those days, the only cylinder players available were the coin-operated ones in local theater lobbies. They were a luxury he couldn't afford. In spite of this, his unique banjo style began to take shape. This resulted, in part, from a baseball accident which had left his right hand arched in a permanent picking position.

Charlie's first outside influence was probably Dana Johnson, the classic banjoist mentioned in the preceding section. Johnson, from nearby Greensboro, was no slouch. His considerable talents enabled him to win first prize in the banjo competition at the 1904 St. Louis Exposition. Poole was also

greatly influenced by Fred Van Eps. Charlie must have owned a number of Van Eps recordings, because he rendered old-time versions of Fred's "Sunset March" and "L'Infanta," as well as "Southern Medley," which was a reworking of Van Eps's popular "Dixie Medley." Even so, Charlie generally avoided buying records. However, he did have a number of favorites. He loved the 78s of Blind Blake, a country blues performer. He also did a lot of listening to a Victor recording of "Cherokee Rag" by Big Chief Henry's *Indian String Band*. Just before his death, Charlie even began listening to Broadway show tunes, although he never had a chance to incorporate them into his own music.

In Poole's mind, the banjo's role in the string band was that of a lead instrument playing a strong accompaniment. Expanding on this concept, Poole's was one of the first rural bands to incorporate "breaks" for certain instruments, instead of featuring the usual ensemble playing. This next tab, taken from Charlie's break on "Flop-Eared Mule," is a good example of this phenomenon. It's also remarkable because it represents a transition from his normal, choppy, chordal, three-finger playing, to a more highly evolved, melody-oriented, essentially Scruggsy sound—and this break dates from 1931!

Flop Eared Mule

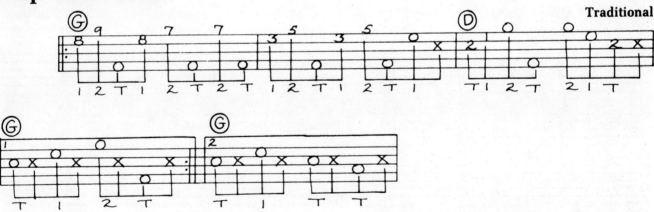

Traditional

Since this was recorded at Charlie's last session, it's impossible to know where his style would have led. But this was apparently the way he preferred to play. Unfortunately, Columbia Records, and the audiences that crammed into the local schoolhouses to hear Poole, wanted him to stick closer to the familiar old-time style that was his trademark. Still, this "uptown" sound was the direction in which he was

headed at the time of his death.

In the last few weeks of his life, it looked like Charlie's success was assured. He was preparing to go to Hollywood to record a movie soundtrack, and even had his ticket in hand. As fate would have it, though, he became ill and died on May 21, 1931, at his sister's home in Spray.

The Soul of Bluegrass

WILL THE CIRCLE BE UNBROKEN
(from *Bluegrass Banjo* by Peter Wernick)
A straightforward version of this Carter Family standard that is a favorite wherever musicians gather to pick. Compare this to Tim Jumper's more basic version on p. 19 in order to see how the left-hand slides, pulls, and hammers combine with right-hand rolls in order to give the Scruggs style its characteristic flavor. Tune to G tuning (gDGBD).

Will the Circle Be Unbroken

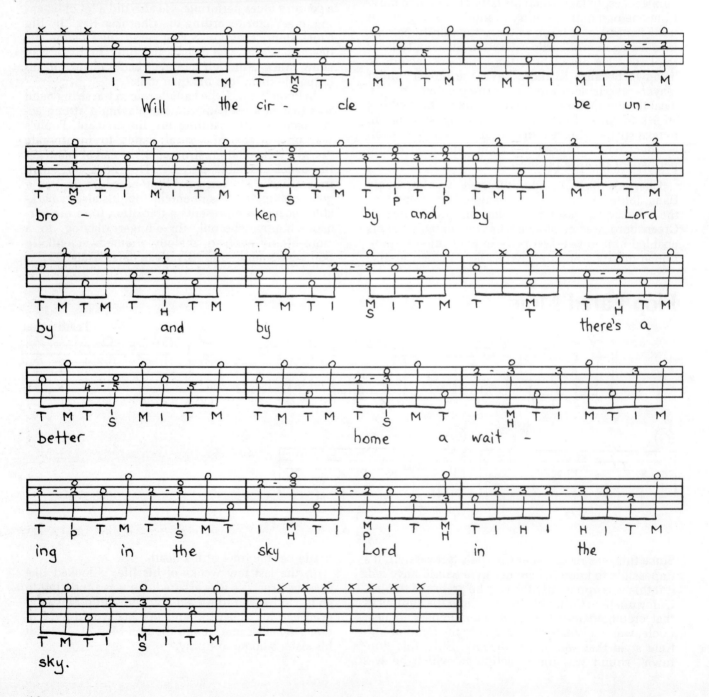

SNUFFY JENKINS' LONESOME ROAD BLUES
(from *Old-Time Mountain Banjo* by Art Rosenbaum)
Both Earl Scruggs and Don Reno have cited Snuffy Jenkins as a formative influence on their own styles—which means, on the whole of bluegrass banjo style. He perfected the three-finger roll, according to Reno, but this solo indicates that he also retained many of the old pre-bluegrass picking patterns in his personal style. Tune to D tuning (f♯DF♯AD).

LONESOME ROAD BLUES

Listen to the original recording of this on *American Banjo, Scruggs Style* Folkways FA 2314, which has several other pre-Bluegrass banjo solos by Jenkins, his cousin Oren Jenkins, Junie Scruggs, J. C. Sutphin and others.

WHAT MAKES A SONG BLUEGRASS?

(from *Bluegrass Songbook* by Peter Wernick)

The soul of bluegrass resides as much or more in singing as it does in instrumental virtuosity, and the banjo player who forgets this not only loses out on a lot of fun, but also finds himself limited professionally. This dialogue between bluegrass musicians is followed by two tried and tested bluegrass standards, "Foggy Mountain Top" and "Footprints in the Snow." The tablature represents the vocal melody; it can be read on strings 2, 3 and 4 of either banjo in G tuning or guitar in standard tuning. Try to make your own instrumental arrangement based on the vocal line; then you'll know you're a real banjo player.

It seems to have to do with two things: the feeling of the story in the song and the kind of instrumental accompaniment that goes with it.

Red Allen: There's no difference between a bluegrass and country song. It's just the way I do it. I just hear a song and if I like it, it sticks in my mind. I'll go home and it will ring in my head and I won't be able to go to sleep. I just feel that it's a grass song.

Bluegrass is sad music. It's always been sad and the people that's never lived it, it'll take them a long time to know what it is.

Do you think a bluegrass musician should have had sorrow in his or her life?

Red Allen: No, but I think they should feel sorrow. Like they should feel up there in Boston, busing people, and blacks and whites hitting each other—that's sorrow right there and they can go out and write a song with sorrow.

James Monroe: A bluegrass song can be anything. You can't classify a bluegrass song, I don't think. Bill Monroe recorded "Danny Boy"—you know how old that song is, it's been done pop and everything else. The way that you would do it could make it your style of bluegrass.

Jimmy Martin: A bluegrass song's got a mandolin, guitar, banjo, and bass fiddle.

Any song can be bluegrass if it's got those instruments?

Jimmy Martin: Yeah. When I look for a song in Nashville they say, "I've got you a good bluegrass song, Jimmy," and they play me a song and say, "This one right here isn't your type, it's a Eddy Arnold song." I say, "Let me hear the lyrics to it; it may be good lyrics and I'll *make* it bluegrass."

Peter Rowan: "The Walls of Time," put a rock-and-roll beat behind it and drums and it would still be bluegrass because it has all of the qualities of a bluegrass song, like that kind of subject matter—death and love, and life is hard, but life is good. I think Bill Monroe once said to me that bluegrass music is like a field holler, just like a blues. It's a basic, direct kind of music. There are some songs that have that quality in any tradition that are sort of bluegrass-type songs.

But to be really a bluegrass song, they have to be treated like a bluegrass song. The variations, like modern bluegrass songs that are Leon Russell tunes and Dylan tunes, they're not really from the bluegrass source but they're adopted into it. They don't thereby become bluegrass tunes, but it becomes a bluegrass treatment of that tune.

Mike Seeger: A bluegrass song, like almost any country song, has to give you the feeling that you're going through it. It's not a conceptualized thing. It tends to be more of a blues idea, one of feeling more than relating an idea or relating an experience.

Jesse McReynolds: It's hard for me to separate what's bluegrass and what's country. It really goes back to what kind of background music you have, whether it's banjo and fiddle and everything, or a country song. Our singing can fit with a country background or most of it could fit with a bluegrass background. We would sing it the same way.

To be a good bluegrass song, you have to keep it up-tempo enough where you can make it fit the banjo good. But you take a song like "Crazy Arms," with the four-four beat they get to it, the western beat, you just can't use a banjo on it. Our banjo picker just goes wild when we do that; he says, "What can I do?" So you got to keep it up-tempo enough. It's hard to get some of them up there that fast and make the words come out right.

Jake Landers: When you write the song, it's hard to tell exactly if it's going to be a bluegrass or a country song. But I think the bluegrass probably has more of a deeper subject involved, and a lot of times tragic. It just mostly tells a story about something, either that you've heard or read about or you've been personally involved in, something that you're familiar with.

Can you write a bluegrass song that's not about cabins in the pines and girls waiting in the mountains? Is it possible to write bluegrass songs about things that happen in the cities, for instance?

Jake Landers: Yeah, I think it's possible to write bluegrass songs about any subject, anything that happens in the big cities or the small towns or the country. I think it needs to be a subject you are fairly familiar with. For instance, I live in a relatively small town and some of the problems involved in some of the larger towns possibly I wouldn't know about.

Everyone likes good lyrics and a good melody, of course. But each artist has his or her own emphasis:

What do you like in a song?
Bill Monroe: One thing about bluegrass, I like to write a true song if I can. I have wrote a good many true songs, like the song of "Uncle Pen" is just as true as you could write a song, and "My Little Georgia Rose" is a true song.

Jimmy Martin: Most of the writers in Nashville think a bluegrass song is the corniest song you can get a hold of, and I disagree with them. "Blue Moon of Kentucky" is not a corny song, it's a good song. "Mule Skinner Blues" is a good lyrics song. "I'll Meet You in Church Sunday Morning," they can't beat the lyrics to it. They think, "Darling come back home, I'm so sad I could cry,"—a real corny song, they think it's bluegrass. But the bluegrass that made a hit, it's a good lyrics song. Take "Tennessee," "Widow Maker," that's as good a lyrics song as a man could find.

Ralph Stanley: I enjoy singing religious music. It has a meaning and a feel that I like. I think a melody has a lot to do with a song too. It can be a good song with a good melody whether the words are too good or not.

John Starling: I think young people are interested in lyrics that make some sense and are relevant to what's happening today. But it's hard to find good lyrics like that and at the same time a good tune. There's a lot of good writers who are writing neat lyrics and I listen to the song but the tune stinks. It would be nice for one person to do, but there's just not that much there in the way of a "socko" chorus or something that makes a good group so that you can do it over and over again and not get tired of it, and also not put the audience to sleep.

Lester Flatt: I always like the story-type songs. They tell you a little something. A lot of the songs you hear today haven't got over four or five words to them. They don't tell you a thing, and it's all over.

Keith Whitley: I just like a song with good strong lyrics, good melody and a story, something that you can sing with feeling.

Carter Stanley had more soul than any other bluegrass singer I ever heard. And that's the same way with his writing. He wasn't afraid to put it down just the way he felt it. I've seen him stand and sing and get so involved in it that tears would just roll, and that's definitely a talent.

Jim McReynolds: You're singing to the people, the hard working-class people, people that's got problems. I think there's gotta be something in that song that says something, that sort of fits their problems. There's something in a song that maybe helps people or does something for them.

Even the big country artists like Loretta Lynn and Charlie Pride, there's some kind of simplicity about their songs. Like the old song, "You Are My Sunshine," there couldn't be anything simpler than "You Are My Sunshine." I remember somebody one time hired us to work for a party over on Long Island and it was a bunch of real big high sophistication people with probably more money than I could dream of seeing. We started asking everybody to sing along with us, and the only song that everybody knew was "You Are My Sunshine."

Keith Whitley

Jesse McReynolds: These country songwriters, when they write a song it's usually a story behind it, you can get a good picture. But a lot of the bluegrass songs we do, especially the up-tempo ones, why it's hard to get a story out of them. And basically I think we need some bluegrass songs that will really compare with what the country singers are doing. I never could get a picture on "Roll In My Sweet Baby's Arms" or "Salty Dog Blues."

Of course now, with the *Country Gentlemen* and some of the new groups, they're venturing out and doing more of a variety of numbers and I think that's going to help it.

Charlie Waller: I suppose everybody has witnessed something that they really like to hear—a sound, with good words, and it makes chill bumps go up you. It can be a good melody or there can be a beautiful poem with good words. But if you've got both of them together you've really got something.

A lot of times the words will carry a song or a lot of times just the tune will. It can have bad words and a good fast-moving thing that you like to hear. I appreciate both and it's getting so that I appreciate better words a whole lot more than I used to. I like intelligent words.

If you listen to our records you won't find too many love songs. There's nothing wrong with sad songs—people like to cry. But usually in country music all the songs are about, "My baby left me, think I'll get a six pack and you take the table and I'll take the chair. Stay unhappy the rest of our lives. . . ." I can't stand those kind of songs.

James Monroe: I like a sad type of song. There's just something about it that turns me on.

Does it make you feel sad?

James Monroe: Yeah, probably does, probably some kind of complex. To me it's a feeling you get. I can't stand a novelty song. I just like something that's got a story to it with a touch of sad.

Red Allen: The songs that I feel is hymns. Now I can sing a religious song and cold chills will run up my back. I can sing anything else and very seldom it does anything to me unless it's a real sad song. I love sad songs. I've lived all my life sad.

Bill and James Monroe, Richard Greene and Peter Rowan

Foggy Mountain Top

Traditional

Medium tempo

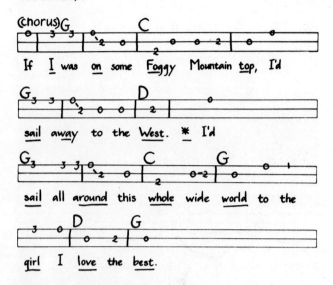

(Chorus)
If I was on some Foggy Mountain top, I'd

sail away to the West. ✱ I'd

sail all around this whole wide world to the

girl I love the best.

If I'd have listened to what mama said
I would not be in here today,
Lying around this old jailhouse
Just wasting my poor life away.

Oh she caused me to weep, she caused me to mourn
She caused me to leave my home.
Oh the lonesome pines and the good old times
I'm on my way back home.

An old tune popularized by the *Carter Family*, and the inspiration behind the name of Flatt and Scruggs' group, the *Foggy Mt. Boys*.

Flatt and Scruggs, *Songs of the Famous Carter Family*/Columbia
The Monroe Brothers, *Feast Here Tonight*/RCA

Footprints In The Snow

Traditional

Bouncy

Some folks like the summertime when they can walk about

Strolling through the meadow green, it's pleasant there's no doubt

But give me the wintertime when the snow is on the ground, I

(chorus)
found her when the snow was on the ground ✱ I

traced her little footprints in the snow ✱ I

found her little footprints in the snow, Lord. God

bless that happy day when my darling lost her way. I

found her when the snow was on the ground.

I went up to see her, there was a big round moon
Her mother said she'd just stepped out
    but would be returning soon.
I found her little footprints
    and I traced them through the snow
I found her when the snow was on the ground.

Now she's up in Heaven, she's with the angel band
I know I'm going to join her in that promised land.
But every time the snow falls, it brings back memories
I found her when the snow was on the ground.

This song dates back to broadsides from the 19th century. Vernon Dalhart and Red Foley recorded popular versions in the 1930s, but since Bill Monroe made it a bluegrass classic in the 1940s, it has been associated with him.

Bill Monroe, *Best of Bill Monroe*/MCA
Bill Monroe, *Country Music Hall of Fame*/MCA
The Osborne Brothers, *Up This Hill and Down*/MCA

GROUND HOG AND DOWN THE ROAD

(from *How to Play Banjo* by Tim Jumper)

Here are two solid songs that should be part of your repertoire. Every good player knows dozens of tunes like this; not flashy, but with individual character. They're fun to play, and serve as a common meeting ground wherever musicians gather to pick and have a good time. Tune to G tuning (gDGBD).

Add these tunes to your repertoire.

Ground Hog

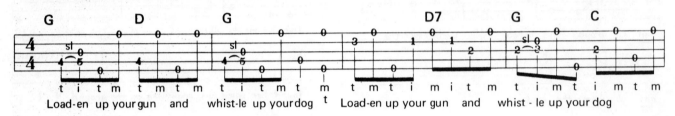

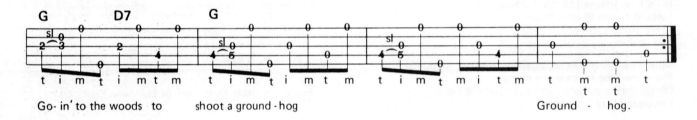

Down The Road

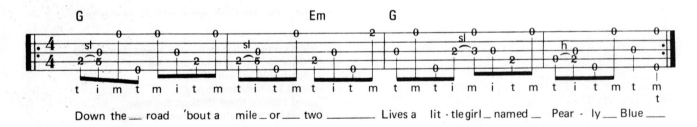

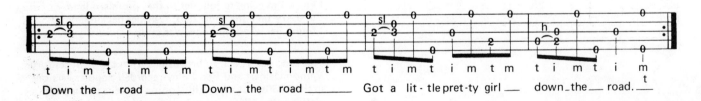

EARL SCRUGGS' MOLLY AND TENBROOKS SOLO

(from *Banjo Songbook* by Tony Trischka)
This section would hardly be complete without a solo from the master himself. Tony Trischka concludes his analysis of Scruggs' style with this transcription of the banjo solo from Bill Monroe's classic racehorse song. Monroe's band at the time included both Scruggs and Lester Flatt; this was the band that once and for all established the definitive bluegras sound. Tune to G (gDGBD).

Taken together, these characteristics indicate that Earl single-handedly standardized a new way of playing the banjo. Though rooted in the past, the sound was smoother than the older three-finger styles. With the addition of the all-important Scruggs licks, it became the perfect complement for the excitingly explosive drive of Monroe's mando-lin. In fact, by 1947, Earl had perfected his style to such an extent that there has since been no need to improve on his formula. His "Molly and Tenbrooks" sounds as contemporary now as it did when it was first recorded—and that's a testament to Earl's remarkable creativity.

Molly and Tenbrooks
(Ten-Brooks and Molly)

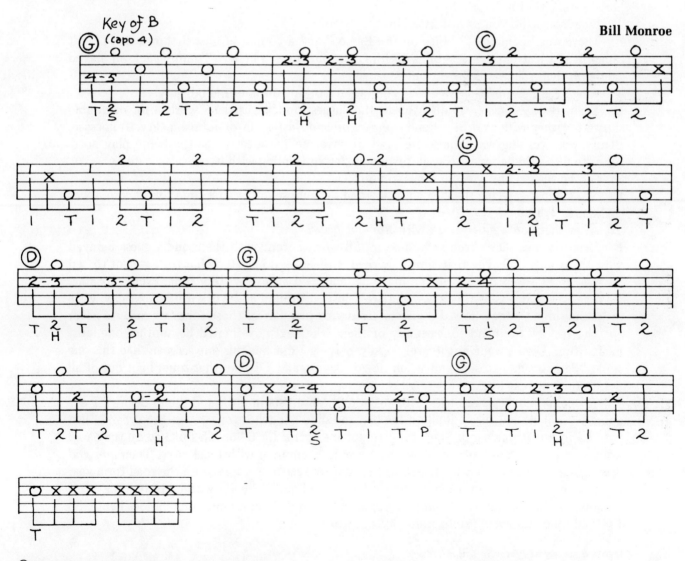

Bill Monroe

BOBBY THOMPSON: INTERVIEW AND KATY HILL SOLO

(from *Melodic Banjo* by Tony Trischka)
Nashville studio musician Bobby Thompson is credited, along with Bill Keith, as a prime innovator of the modern melodic style. The interview is followed by his arrangement of "Katy Hill," a fiddle tune that is sometimes also called "Sally Johnson." Tune to G tuning (gDGBD).

Tony: When did you start playing banjo?

Bobby: It was probably '51 or '52.

T: What first interested you in playing?

B: A friend of mine started playing guitar and I heard "Foggy Mountain Breakdown." I didn't even know what the instrument was, but I found out and I decided I'd try that.

T: Did you have any lessons?

B: No I just picked it up, most of it from records.

T: Who did you listen to back then besides Scruggs? Did you listen to Don Reno?

B: Yeah. Those were the only two I knew of that played.

T: What was your first professional job?

B: I worked with two or three groups, but playing with Carl Story was the first really professional job I had.

T: What songs did you record with him?

B: There was "Banjolina," "Fire on the Banjo," and a couple of gospel things that I can't remember. I just did one session with him . . . four tunes. I believe Tommy Jackson played fiddle on them. That was '57 or '58.

T: Was it right around this time that you began working on your melodic style?

B: Yeah. Benny Sims (a fiddler) made the suggestion. We used to work a lot of double shows together with Carl Story and *Bonny Lou and Buster* out of Johnson City, Tennessee. Benny was working with them. He kind of gave me the idea to see the banjo play note-for-note like a fiddle tune. So I sat down and started fiddling with it.

T: Did he suggest any specific tunes to you?

B: No. He just gave me the idea and I worked on it myself. The first tune I worked out was "Arkansas Traveler."

T: After that you went to work with *Jim and Jesse*?

B: Right. It must have been sometime in '58 when I went with them and I guess I stayed with them until '60. The first time I worked with Jesse, no matter what time we got to bed he was up at seven o'clock in the morning, and he'd always write a tune, every morning. He'd get me and Vassar Clements, and we'd just sit around and work it up. Next day was a different tune. . . . and now, I'd give anything for just part of those tunes we did. We never got the rest of the band to learn any of them—the next day there'd be another one. Just having fun. Then I went in the army. Only playing I did was this one sergeant had this one tune, "San Antonio Rose," and when he got drunk, and I'd play that tune, I got out of all details for the next week.*

When I came out, I played bass with a group for about six months and then I decided I was going to quit it, and threw it all on the bed and didn't touch it for two or three years. I just worked in a machine shop. Then the bug got me again. In '64 or '65 I picked up the banjo again and played lead guitar a little bit. I was just jamming with local guys. Then *Jim and Jesse* got me to go back with them, so I moved to Nashville. I stayed on the road for a year or so with them, then got tired of the road again and quit. I finally worked into doing a few sessions. Then I found out I was going to starve if I didn't play something besides banjo. So I picked up guitar and got into some rhythm work.

*Quote courtesy of *Bluegrass Unlimited*.

Bobby Thompson with *Jim and Jesse* and Vassar Clements.

T: What kind of music were you listening to back then?

B: I used to listen to a little bit of everything. I used to listen to a lot of jazz, then I just completely lost interest in it.

T: When did you first hear Bill Keith?

B: I can't remember the first time I heard Bill play. . . . maybe it was on the Opry. The first tune I heard him play was "Sailor's Hornpipe," and I thought it was great.

T: How did you come to meet him?

B: A friend of mine, Don Limeburger, was working with Bill Monroe at one time, and he first told me about Keith, and I'd never heard him play. So then Bill called me one day, and I wasn't even knowing who he was, because I wasn't really keeping up with it back then. I had just picked the banjo back up and started messing with it again. So he came down and we just sat around and picked awhile. Bill went farther with the melodic style than I had, 'cause I'd kind of stalled out and pretty much forgotten about it. I know there was two years there where I didn't much touch it. I know everybody always asks me this, and I really don't have no good answer. I don't know if he got anything from me or if he just run up on it same as I did.

T: How about those descending blues runs and scales?

B: I got hung up on that for a few years and never got to use it 'til we did *Area Code 615*. I guess that was the period I was really into it.

T: Those runs involved taking guitar licks and applying them to the banjo?

B: Well, you'd hear a run that maybe you couldn't do on banjo, but you could work something around it. I kind of got into the habit of hearing a lick enough to halfway remember it, then sitting down and coming up with something around it so I wouldn't be doing the same thing. I picked that up from a lot of the studio guys I was working with.

T: You like working in the studio?

B: Yeah, I really do. The money's good. I'd say that. There's always variety. Working with a regular band you've usually got a show worked up. You do the same tunes night after night, and you might change one or two songs and that's about it. In the studio, you never know what you're going to do until you get there. When I go in I don't know if I'm playing guitar, banjo, or what. It really keeps it interesting. You have to be constantly coming up with new things to keep working, and you're always around new ideas. That's what I enjoy about it.

T: Who have you listened to and learned from in the Nashville studios?

B: A lot of people. I guess Wayne Moss, Grady Martin, Charlie McCoy—I got a lot of blues stuff from Charlie. And a lot of the steel players—Lloyd Green, Hal Rugg, Weldon Myrick.

T: What else have you learned in the studio?

B: You've got to cut commercial records, and then when you kind of get off the track, they calm you down and you begin to realize that you're selling to the public, not musicians.

T: Getting back to the melodic style, what would you suggest to someone who's just getting into it?

B: I think if you're going to learn banjo you should learn the basic Scruggs and Reno style along with the other, because there are so many types of music where that's all you need, basic licks fit best. With melodic stuff there's no set rolls or patterns, you just have to figure out a way you can get the notes and adapt the roll to get it. And that gets pretty confusing on some of the fiddle tunes. You'll go through them and there may be five notes different. You have to remember which one you're playing. That happens to me. I'll get two or three tunes confused. I'll get into it and then realize I'm going the wrong way and try to get out of it and can't. I think it's a style you have to play enough to do without thinking about it.

Bobby Thompson

Katy Hill

Traditional
Bobby Thompson
Arranged and adapted by Area Code 615

Key of G
Part A

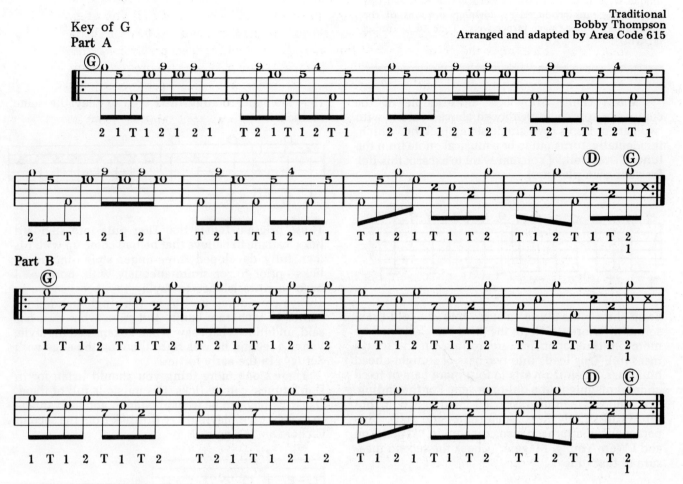

© 615 Music. All Rights Reserved. Used by Permission.

As played on Area Code 615 *Trip in the Country*, Polydor Records 24-4025

DON RENO'S MAMA DON'T ALLOW
(from *Banjo Songbook* by Tony Trischka)
Another classic bluegrass banjo player is Don Reno. His unique style is a composite of Scruggs-like rolls and fast single-string runs produced by down-up motions of the thumb and index finger respectively. Tune to G tuning (gDGBD).

"Mama Don't Allow" is an example of the composite approach mentioned above. It starts with two bars of Don's own single string picking, which, incidentally, turns out to be a musical quote from the tune "Silver Bell." (You may want to excerpt this lick for your own playing.)

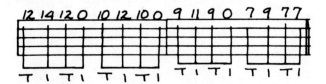

From here, the tune moves into an old-time-sounding chordal lick (in the third bar), followed by more old-time open forward rolling (in the fourth measure). This leads into two bars of straight-ahead bluegrass. Then it reverts to four more bars of fixed chordal playing in the old-time vein. For the ending, Don chooses a bluegrassy left-hand position, but throws in strictly Renoesque right-hand rolls. This personalized approach also crops up in "When You and I Were Young, Maggie." Check the second measure of that tune:

Here's a more Scruggsified way to play the same melody:

These original twists that Don puts into standard licks lead me to believe that he had come up with his own fully developed three-finger style—including licks—prior to, or simultaneously with, Scruggs. I have some resistance to saying this because we've always considered Earl to be the single-handed inventor of bluegrass banjo. But from what Don has said, and from what I saw when I examined his style, I have a feeling he was right there on the edge with Scruggs in the early forties.

There's one more thing you should listen for in Don's tunes: catchy licks. His music is full of them. Usually, they can be transplanted to good advantage in to your own playing. Try this lick from the second C chord in "Maggie":

Remember, Don has a lot to offer. So when you tire of all those ascending and descending melodic runs, you should give him a try.

Mama Don't Allow

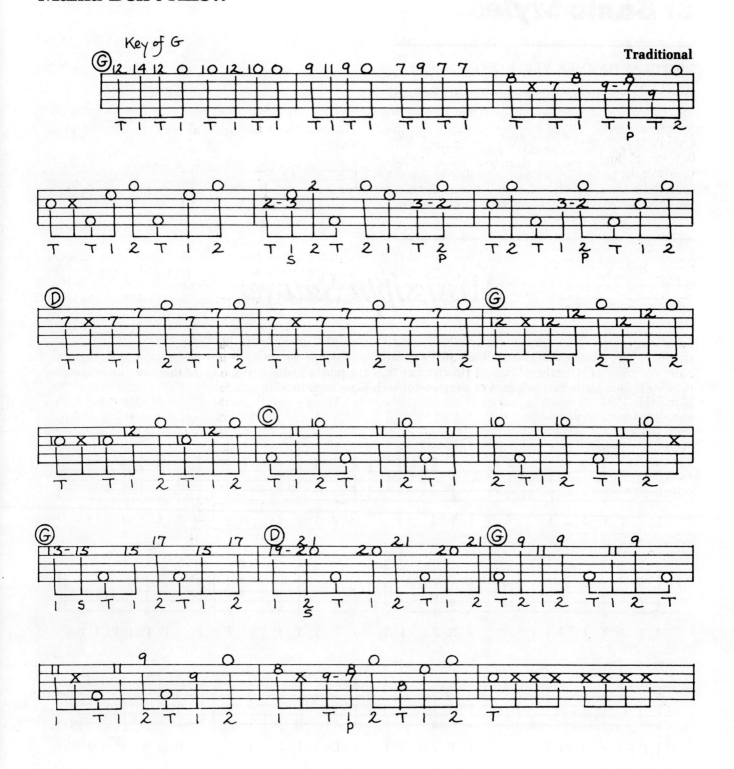

The Infinite Variety of Banjo Styles

TWO CLAWHAMMER VERSIONS OF MISSIS-SIPPI SAWYER

(This page: from *Clawhammer Banjo* by Miles Krassen)
Tune to double D tuning aDADE. Can also be read in double C tuning gCGCD—see p. 34.

Next page: from *John Burke's Book of Old-Time Fiddle Tunes for Banjo*. Tune to standard C tuning (gCGBD).

Both versions are inspired by Wade Ward's melody, yet each is true to the author's personal banjo style. Note how Burke more often uses the basic frailing rhythm, and how the difference in choice of tuning results in different possibilities for hammering and pulling.

Mississippi Sawyer

Both George and Wade Ward have recorded good banjo versions of this classic fiddle tune. Wade had a great way of using the Galax lick in the second part. In the tablature below, notice how the plucked first string is fitted into the second part. This is a very useful technique in D tuning.

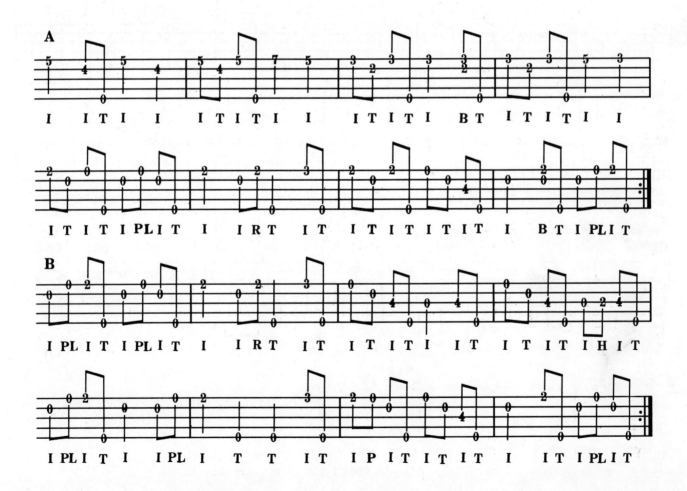

Mississippi Sawyer

from WADE WARD

G C G B D

A-Part

B-Part

A'-Part

B'-Part

Reference: Folkways: Wade Ward &
Roscoe Holcomb, FA2365

The A and B sections here correspond
closely to the record, while the other
parts are my own.

(This page: from *John Burke's Book of Old-Time Fiddle Tunes for Banjo*. Tune to G modal tuning gDGCD.
Next page: from *Melodic Banjo* by Tony Trischka. Tune to G tuning gDGBD).

This fast-moving fiddle tune of Irish origin is a challenge to play on the banjo no matter which style you choose. Notice how the choice of modal tuning in Burke's setting makes for a more lonesome, archaic sound.

Paddy On The Turnpike

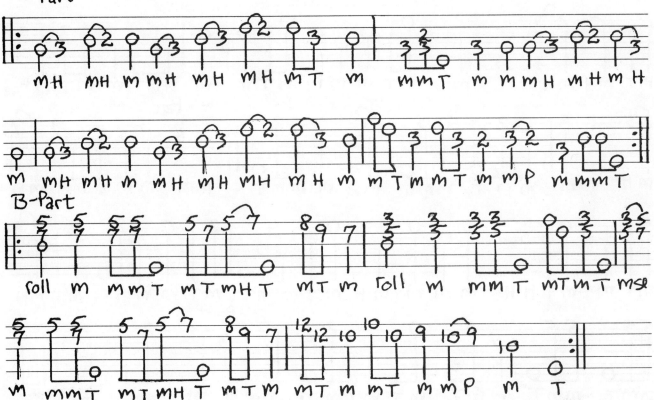

Reference:
Old Time Banjo Project: Elektra, Elk.276

Though I have set this tune in the key of G, it is played on the record in the key of D. I have found only a few fiddlers who play the tune in D. Most play it in G. This setting is almost half-made up of "hammered-on" notes. This is rare in Clawhammer, but as long as you hammer hard and keep the notes clean it will sound pretty good.

Paddy On The Turnpike

Key of G
Part A

Traditional
Arranged and adapted by Tony Trischka

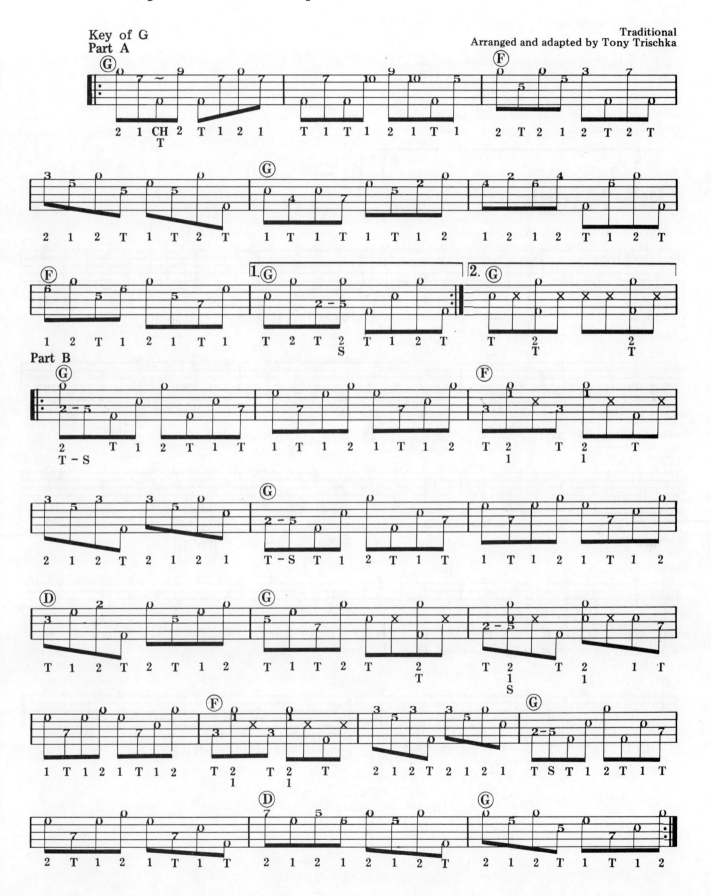

TWO BLUEGRASS VERSIONS OF LITTLE MAGGIE
(This page: from *Bluegrass Banjo* by Peter Wernick.
Next page: Ralph Stanley's version from *Banjo Songbook*
by Tony Trischka. Tune to G tuning gDGBD for both versions.)

Each version differs considerably in the way the melody is
phrased, with different choices of rolls, pulls, slides, hammers and rests, and even with choice of string on which a
given melody note is played. The sum total of such small
distinctions can make one player sound completely different than another.

Little Maggie

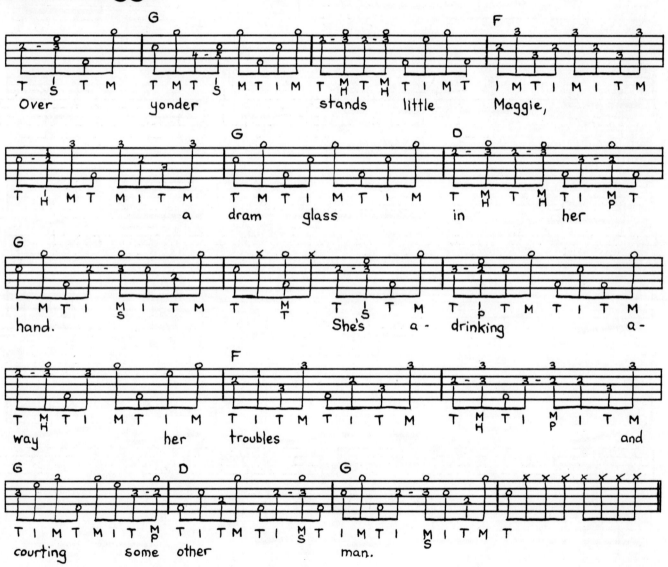

Little Maggie

capo 5
Key of C

Ralph Stanley

59

BLUEGRASS AND CLAWHAMMER VERSIONS OF JOHN HARDY

(This page: from *Bluegrass Banjo* by Peter Wernick.
Next page: from *Clawhammer Banjo* by Miles Krassen.
Tune to G tuning gDGBD for both versions.)
Notice how Wernick's version makes frequent use of the "blue note" on the third fret of the third string, a sound

that comes from the blues influence on bluegrass. Krassen's setting avoids that note completely, moving on the second and fourth frets in order to bring out sounds that belong more to the world of dulcimers and Celtic fiddlers. This Carter Family song was the inspiration for Dylan's "John Wesley Harding."

John Hardy

John Hardy

John Hardy is probably best known as a ballad and has been recorded as such many times. A fine version was recorded in the 1920's by Clarence Ashley accompanying himself on the banjo. Around Galax the melody is often used as a dance tune. Sometimes it is played in A. Wade Ward and Charlie Higgins used to play a fine version of John Hardy at Parson's Auction on Saturday's in Galax. Some banjo players use a minor tuning for this tune. But the advantage of playing it in standard G tuning is demonstrated by the pull-off from the first fret on the second string as in measure one which can be used very effectively.

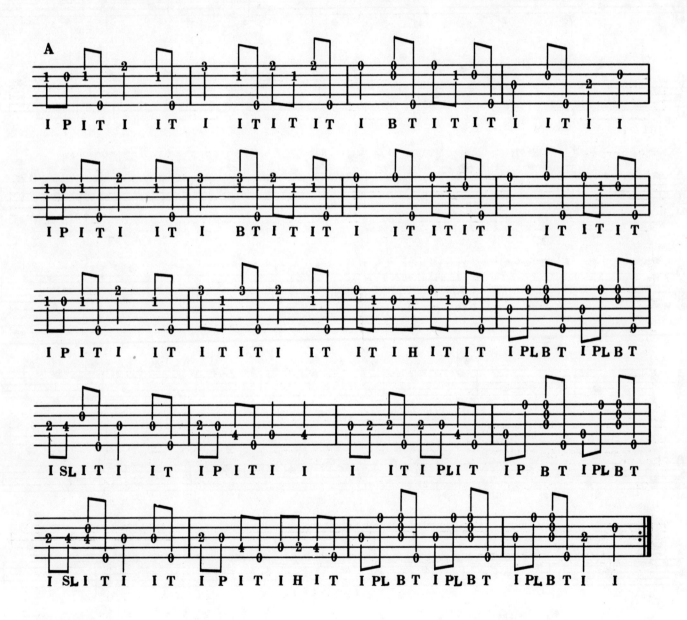

ANDANTE BY FERNANDO SOR
(from *Classical Banjo* by Al Jeffrey)

In conclusion, a treat for working up your note-reading. Fernando Sor (1778-1839) was one of the great com- posers for classical guitar, and even his simpler instruction- al pieces have, like this one, great melodic charm and com- positional togetherness. Read this banjo adaptation in standard C tuning (gCGBD).